EXPLORING CATHEDRALS
A Short Guide

Worcester Cathedral.

John Wittich

PRYOR PUBLICATIONS
WHITSTABLE, WALSALL
AND WINCHESTER

MEMBER OF
INDEPENDENT PUBLISHERS GUILD

First published by Norheimsund Books and Cards,
Burton Latimer, Northants. 1992

Second, revised, edition 1996

© John Wittich

St. Paul's From Across The River, 1872.
Water colour by T. C. Dibdin

© 1996 Pryor Publications
75 Dargate Road, Yorkletts, Whitstable,
Kent CT5 3AE, England.
Tel. & Fax: (01227) 274655
Specialists in Facsimile Reproductions

Drawings by Charles Bird
Drawing of Wakefield Cathedral by John Cox

ISBN 0 946014 58 2

A CIP Record for this book is available from the British Library

Printed by Oyster Press, Whitstable, Kent
01227 772605

DEDICATION

This second, revised, edition is dedicated to Phil and Mary Mason who bravely published the first edition in 1992. Now due to circumstances beyond their control, they have released the copyright to me. Thank you both for your generosity and faith in this title.

John Wittich
Feast of St. Paul the Apostle
London, 1996

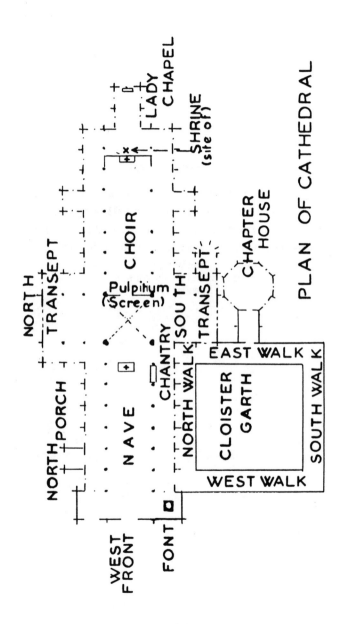

ABBEYS AND CATHEDRALS - a number of cathedrals were monastic establishments, and have retained some of the domestic buildings from that time, albeit as ruins in many cases.

Visit: Canterbury - Chichester - Gloucester - Hereford - Salisbury - Wells - Worcester.

ALTAR RAILS - were ordered by Archbishop William Laud in the 17th century in order to protect the altar from abuse by animals. Before the rails were erected a houseling cloth was held in front of the communicants to prevent crumbs of the Sacred Bread falling to the ground.

ALTARS - is the altar or holy table where the Eucharist is regularly celebrated. In earlier times the altar was often erected over the tomb of a saint or benefactor. Hanging over the altar is a cloth whose colours reflect the Seasons of the Church. The high altar of Lichfield is over seven hundred years old.

ARCADING - a series of arches whose shape or form varies according to the time of its construction.

Visit: Norwich   Durham   Lincoln   York   Bristol   Chelmsford
       12thc   12thc   13thc   14thc   16thc   19thc

ARCHITECTURAL STYLES - the following is a rough guide to the dates of the various styles:-

Norman (Romanesque)	1050-1150
Gothic Early English	1150-1250
Decorated	1250-1350
Perpendicular	1350-1550
Renaissance	17th century
Neo-classical	18th century
Neo-Gothic	19th century

BATIKS - method of printing coloured designs on textiles by waxing parts that are not to be dyed.

Visit: Winchester where they hang as banners during festival times.

BRASSES - more correctly, monumental or memorial brasses are flat sheets of a metal called latten that is made up of roughly two thirds copper and one third zinc with a small amount of lead and tin. It was originally made in Germany, primarily in and around Cologne, and was also known as Cullen from the name of that city. The sheets are engraved with figures representing the person or persons buried in the grave over which they have been placed.

Visit: Carlisle - Bishop Bell, 1496 with a triple canopy.
      Chichester - heart c.1510, Bishop Day 1536, William Bradbridge civilian with wife 1592.
      Ely - Bishop Goodrick, 1554 and Dean Tyndall 1614.
      Exeter - Sir Peter Courtenay with canopy 1409, Canon Langeton priest in cope and kneeling 1413.
      Hereford - Bishop Trilleck with canopy 1360, Priest in cope in head of cross c. 1360, Dean Frowsetoure in cope within a canopy 1529.
      Manchester - Bishop Stanley of Ely 1515.
      Oxford - various students in academic dress dating from the 16th century

Inlaid Brass Monument of Eleanor Bohun, wife to Thomas of Woodstock, Duke of Gloucester. — Died 1399.

Brass of Sir Thomas Bulieu.

St. Albans - Abbot Delamere c. 1360, various monks 15th and 16th century.
Salisbury - Bishop Wyvil half effigy in castle 1375, Bishop Geste 1578.
York - Archbishop Grenefeld 1315, Elizabeth Eynns half effigy 1585.

CAPITALS - at the top of columns that support the arches and are often carved either with foliage or scenes from Life (telling a moral story), or simply illustrating a biblical scene.

Visit: Carlisle - whose capitals depict the months of the year.
Wells - includes "The Apple Pickers", or are they scrumping (stealing)?
Southwell - the Chapter House is full of naturalistic foliage.

Early English Capitals, York Cathedral.

Capital, Wells.

CARRELS - cubicles in the cloisters where the monks studied and wrote manuscripts.
Visit: Chester and Gloucester

CATHEDRA - the Bishop's throne from where he sat and taught his clergy - a tradition whereby the Rabbi gathered around his students.
Visit: Durham - whose 14th century *cathedra* is the highest in Christendom.

CEILINGS - a flat, wooden, inside surface of the roof.
Visit; Ely - painted in the nineteenth century and recently restored.
Peterborough - dating from the thirteenth century and unique in England.

CHAIRS - the congregations mostly either stood or knelt during the services, but there were special chairs in some cathedrals, viz. Canterbury's St.Augustine's Chair used for the enthronement of Archbishops. Named after the First Archbishop of Britain, it dates from the 13th century. Portsmouth has a Corporation Chair, dating from 1694, and it is used by the Lord Mayor of Portsmouth when he attends the cathedral on official occasions.

CHAPELS - part of the building with a separate altar. Most cathedrals have at least one side chapel set aside for those who wish to spend a short time quietly in prayer or meditation. There is usually a notice asking visitors to respect the purpose of the chapel and not to enter unless they wish to use it "properly". Chantry chapels are ones that have been erected over a burial within the church building. In Pre-Reformation times mass was often said for the repose of the donor. Other chapels may be dedicated to particular saints, in particular the Blessed Virgin Mary (The Lady Chapel), while others form Regimental Chapels for local and county branches of the Armed Forces.
Visit: Lady Chapels - Hereford - St.Albans - Wells - York
Regimental Chapels - Canterbury - Guildford - Leicester - Sheffield

CHAPTER - in charge of the running of the cathedral is the Dean whose staff of canons assist him and are known as The Chapter from the time when the Abbot of the monasteries called a daily meeting of the brethren in the Chapter House.
Visit: Southwell late 13th century - Wells 1263 - Gloucester in whose chapter house William the Conqueror ordered the writing of the Doomsday survey of 1086 - Worcester 1140.

CHOIR - part of the church set aside for the singers, and where in monastic times the monks would assemble to sing the various offices. Many of the medieval cathedrals have stalls (seats) with misericords which derive their name from the Latin misericordia, 'pity'. By resting against them the monks and nuns relaxed their bodies during the services.

Visit; Carlisle - with some of the finest medieval stalls in England.
- Chichester - dating from the fourteenth century. Ask to be shown the "longest kiss in history".
- Durham - "late example" dating from the 17th century.
- Ely - 14th century with some delightful misericords.
- Gloucester - another 14th century example with the wooden effigy of Duke Robert the eldest son of William the Conqueror between the stalls.
- Norwich - 15th century complete with misericords.
- St.Paul's, London - the 17th century choir stalls are by Grinling Gibbons.
- Winchester - date from 1308.

CLOCKS - were rare in medieval churches, the times of the services being announced by the ringing of the bells.
Visit: St.Paul's, London - Salisbury (dating from c 1386) - Wells (14th century with its jousting knights and figure of Jack Bladifer).

CLOISTERS - in monastic times the cloisters were used by the monks and nuns as a place of prayer and meditation when not in the church. They were constructed as a covered way around a quadrangle, or garth. Usually the garth was a grassed over area, and was not intended to be used as a burial ground.
Visit: Gloucester which is of outstanding magnificence and is complete with lavatorium and recesses for towels. The West Walks has a fine set of carrels, in the East Walk there are markings on the stone seats for a game played by the novices.

CLOSE - around the cathedral building is often an (en)closed area where the staff of the cathedral live.

Visit: Canterbury - whose buildings include the King's School.
- Salisbury - where the cathedral is surrounded by houses dating from medieval and later times.
- Wells - that houses the Vicar's Choral complete with their own chapel and communal hall.

CONSISTORY COURT - a court under the jurisdiction of a bishop where misdemeanours of clergy and parishes can be heard - and judged.
Visit: Chester - oaken screens, seats and table date from 1636
- Leicester - Southwark.

CROSS - the sign of Christianity symbolising the means of death of Our Lord and Saviour Jesus Christ. Crosses were often erected by the side of the roads. Missionaries, and other priests would proclaim the Good News (Gospel) of the Lord to the populace. In the north-east corner of St.Paul's (London) churchyard there was erected an outdoor pulpit that became known as "Paul's Cross". It was pulled down in the 17th century, but not before Papal Edicts and punishments were proclaimed from it.

CRYPTS - defined as an underground, windowless, area the crypt today is often used for exhibitions of a permanent or temporary nature. In places such as Canterbury where there are windows, chapels have been laid out. York* Minster's restorations in recent years have opened up the crypt more fully to provide an excellent museum.

Visit: Canterbury - the largest 12th century crypt in the world
Gloucester - 11th century with its squat, ponderous columns
London, St. Paul's - the largest in Europe.

*Minster = a large church. Originally a place of "ministering" of the Gospel over which a church was later erected.

DEANS - after William the Conqueror defeated the English at the Battle of Hastings in 1066 many of the Norman Bishops became deeply involved in Parliament and Politics. Most of them rose to positions of power where their duties took them away from their cathedrals. The result was the Senior Canon became the Dean, and the responsibility of running the cathedral was handed over to him. Most modern foundation cathedrals elect a Provost whose responsibilities are the same. Bishops have no rights over the cathedral's organisation and are, normally, invited to attend services rather than having the absolute right to do so.

EMBROIDERY - embroidered cloths were a prominent feature of a medieval house decorations. The church uses embroidery to produce banners to be carried in processions, or displayed on the pillars of the church.
Visit: Coventry - Exeter - Salisbury - Wells - Canterbury.

ENTRANCE FEES - many cathedrals charge a fee which may be compulsory or voluntary to assist in the running of the church buildings. At Canterbury there is an entrance fee to the Precincts which includes the cathedral.

FLOOR TILES - the revival in the nineteenth century of the use of encaustic tiles to cover parts of the church brought back a medieval practice. A number of medieval tiles have survived and can be seen making up pavements in various cathedrals. The floor tiles in the library of Lichfield Cathedral date from the 13th century.

FONTS - a receptacle containing holy water that is used for the Sacrament of Baptism when a person, young or old, is formally admitted into the Christian Church. The Canon Law of the Church of England states:- ".. the font shall stand as near to the principal entrance as conveniently may be..." (Canon F2) Visit: Hereford - Canterbury - Portsmouth - Wells - Winchester (with scenes from the life of St.Nicholas of Myra) - St.Paul's London - in north transept, and a second, much smaller, in the crypt in the Chapel of the Order of the British Empire.

Font, Winchester.

FRESCOES AND MURAL WALL PAINTINGS - frescoes are painted on the plaster while it is still wet, and murals are painted after the plaster has dried.

Visit: St.Albans - Canterbury - Lincoln (see St. Blaise Patron Saint of Woolcombers in the Russell Chantry Chapel by Duncan Grant 1958) - Carlisle (depicting the lives of St.Anthony, St. Augustine and St.Cuthbert) - Rochester (choir with a "Wheel of Fortune").

GATEHOUSES - in the protecting wall that surrounds The Close they were to both guard and protect the inhabitants.
Visit: Norwich - Canterbury - Salisbury - Wells - Bristol - Worcester - Gloucester.

HOSPITALITY - always played an important part in the life of the monasteries in the Middle Ages, and continues to do so today with the provision in many cathedrals of rest rooms and restaurant facilities.

I.H.S. - the most satisfactory and interesting explanation of this symbol is that the letters IHS are a contraction, or monogram, of the sacred name of Jesus. It is difficult to find out exactly when this device was first used. Emperor Constantine is said to have suggested I(n) H(oc) S(igho) as being the sign "I will conquer". It has also been understood to be the initials from Jesus Hominum Salvator, that is, "Jesus Saviour of Mankind". In the Middle Ages it was widely used by the Dominican Order and later adopted by the Society of Jesus (Jesuits).

LECTERNS - a reading desk for supporting heavy books (i.e. the Holy Bible) and often in the form of an eagle. The bird stands on a round ball, said to represent the world, whose beak is often open. In medieval days visitors were encouraged to leave monetary offerings in the beak. This safeguarded the money from being stolen. Eagles are said to be able to fly highest in the sky, so taking the petitions of the people heavenwards, and can fly the longest distances without a rest.

Visit: Newcastle - Peterborough - Southwell (all with medieval lecterns) Wells - York (both with seventeenth century examples) - St.Paul's,London (provided in 1720 and made by Jacob Sutton for £241).

LIBRARIES AND ARCHIVES - from early times cathedrals were sources of education and learning. Most still have extensive libraries and records and most, though not all, allow visitors.
Visit: Canterbury - Salisbury (who own a copy of the Magna Carta) - St.Paul's London - Lincoln (also has a Magna Carta) - Lichfield (most precious possession are the Gospels of St.Chad) - Manchester - Chelmsford - Rochester.

'LINCOLN IMP' - one day the devil was out for a ride on the wind when he saw the new cathedral being built on the top of the hill in Lincoln. Being of an inquisitive nature he looked into the church, sat down on the top of one of the columns and went to sleep! He never woke up. He was turned to stone and can still be seen "resting" in the "Angel Choir" at the east end of the Cathedral church. "And he grins at the people who gaze so solemnly".

LITURGICAL COLOURS - colours in churches and cathedrals are used to denote the festivals and seasons of the Church.

        White   Christmas - Easter - Ascension - the Blessed Virgin Mary - saints who were not martyred.

        Red   Pentecost (*Whitsun) - saints who were martyrs.

        Green   the colour of Creation - and used throughout the Sundays after Pentecost.

Purple or blue seasons of sorrow and repentance i.e. Advent, (the Sundays before Christmas) - Lent and funerals.

Many cathedrals and churches use white today for funerals.

*Originally Pentecost Sunday was called White Sunday from the clothes worn by the catechumens who were being confirmed.

MASTER MASONS - a combination of architect + surveyor + clerk of the works they supervised the building of the cathedral. Among the best known are William of Sens, and his successor William the Englishman who rebuilt Canterbury cathedral after the disastrous fire of 1067.

MITRES - are worn by Archbishops and Bishops and are usually triangular in shape.

MODERN CATHEDRALS - Coventry - designed by Sir Basil Spence and built at a right-angle to the ruins of the 14th century parish church cathedral that was destroyed in 1940 by "enemy action".

Guildford - an entirely new cathedral designed by Sir Edward Maufe and built between 1936 and 1961.

Liverpool - the red sandstone building, designed by Sir Giles Gilbert Scott, was built between 1904 and 1978.

MONASTIC ORDERS AND THEIR CATHEDRALS -

AUGUSTINIAN CANONS - their Rule was based on the 109th Letter of St. Augustine of Hippo. They were all priests and were not confined to living within a precinct but "serviced" parishes throughout the dioceses viz. Bristol - Carlisle - Oxford - Southwark.

BENEDICTINES - St.Benedict wrote the Rule in the 5th century, and almost all other Orders either adopted or adapted it for their own. The Order is one of great learning, many universities and schools owe their origin to the Order viz. Canterbury - Chester - Coventry - Durham - Ely - Gloucester - Norwich - Peterborough - Rochester - St.Albans - Winchester - Worcester.

SECULAR CANONS - were to serve the needs of a cathedral or collegiate church. Strictly speaking they were not monks but lived a communal life eating in common hall, taking a vow of celibacy, under a form of discipline, viz. Chester - Chichester - Exeter - Hereford - Lichfield - Lincoln - St.Paul's, London - Ripon - Salisbury - Wells - York.

MONUMENTS - on the wall of nearly all the cathedrals are memorials and monuments to men and women who have played their part in the history of the city and the cathedral. They make interesting reading and often provided an insight into the trade and professions from the past. One of the most famous memorials, found above his tomb in St.Paul's,London is that of Sir Christopher Wren. It reads :-

"Si monumentum requiris, circumspice"
(If you seek his monument, look around you)

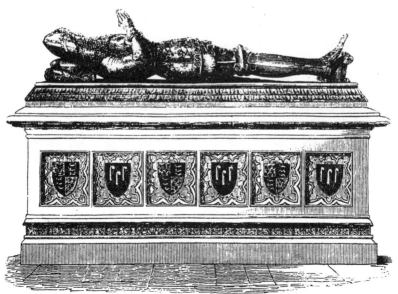

Monument of Edward the Black Prince, in Canterbury Cathedral.

NAVE - here the general public were allowed when the building was monastic. In front of the pulpitium (the screen that divided nave from choir), stood the Jesus Altar at which the Eucharist was celebrated. For the people feeling unwell or getting old, there was seating around the wall, hence the saying "the weakest to the wall".

    Visit: Canterbury - Chichester - Ely - Exeter - Hereford -   Lincoln
        *Newcastle - Peterborough - Rochester - Southwell.
        *the nave here is narrower than the side aisles which had 18
        chantry chapels in them in former times.

ORGANS - this fine instrument has its origins in the 3rd century B.C. and by the time of the eighth century had been introduced into Christian worship. In the tenth century Winchester's boasted over 400 pipes and 26 bellows. The records of Worcester show that in the fourteenth century payments were made to a musician to "thump the organs, teach quire boys, and to instruct any of the monks who wished to learn the art of organ thumping". Durham had one in the thirteenth century, and at the time of the Dissolution of the Monasteries in 1539. Organ cases form a prominent feature of most cathedrals, and are naturally visible to the visitor. The pipework may also be seen but seldom, if ever, visited , the organ loft being out of bounds to all except authorised personnel.

    Visit: To see organ cases of the ....

        17th century: Bristol - Durham - Gloucester - Newcastle - Oxford - St.Paul's, London.

        18th century: Wakefield

        19th century: Chichester - Ely - Lincoln - Portsmouth - Ripon - Rochester - Winchester - York - Bangor - St.Asaph.

        20th century: Bradford - Chelmsford - Lichfield - Guildford - Liverpool Peterborough - St.Albans.

"Father" Henry Willis was one of the most prolific organ builders of the 19th century and his work can be seen at Canterbury - Gloucester - Hereford - Lincoln - St.Paul's London - Salisbury - Truro and Winchester, whose organ was exhibited at the Great Exhibition of 1851 in London's Hyde Park.

PAINTINGS - medieval churches and cathedrals were colourful with wall paintings, stained glass, and vestments, etc. In an attempt to brighten up the buildings, and at the same time provide a focal point of prayer and meditation several cathedrals have hung paintings on the walls.
Visit: St.Paul's London - with Holman Hunt's "Light of the World".
    Chichester - where on the altar in the south east corner of the church
    stands Graham Sutherland's "Mary Magdalene meets Christ in the
    Garden".

PARISH CHURCH CATHEDRALS - between 1847 and 1927 fifteen parish churches were "raised to the dignity" of becoming a   cathedral. Half of them have been "added to" with modern extensions in order to cope with the large congregations that can be expected from time to time.

Visit: Birmingham (1905) - Blackburn (1926) - Bradford (1919) - Bury St. Edmunds (1914) - Chelmsford (1914) - Coventry (1918) - Derby (1927) - Leicester (1926) - Manchester (1847) - Newcastle (1878) - Portsmouth (1927) - Sheffield (1914) - Southwark (1905) - Southwell (1884) - Truro (1887) - Wakefield (1887).

Wakefield Cathedral.

PILGRIMS - PAST AND PRESENT - what is a pilgrimage, who went on them? Do they still happen today? The answer is that a pilgrimage is a journey to a sacred place, and they certainly still regularly take place today. Originally the primary destination for Christians was the Holy Land, to places associated with Christ and His Mother and later the tombs of the early saints of the Church. At the collapse of the Roman Empire these places were closed to pilgrims, and it wasn't until the 12th and 13th centuries, with the advent of the Crusades, that they were revived. In the 12th century St. Francis of Assisi devised another form of devotions that of the Stations of the Cross whereby images, displayed on the walls of the church, drew attention to the Passion, Death and Resurrection of Our Lord. Many people still walk the "Way of the Cross" in their own churches during the period of Lent each year.

In England two of the greatest shrines, St. Thomas Becket, in Canterbury Cathedral and Little Walsingham, in Norfolk both attracted vast crowds of pilgrims to them. Shrines developed their own cults, attracted great wealth both to the town or city, as well as the site of the shrine itself. In 1498 Wynkyn de Worde compiled the first pilgrimage handbook - "Informacion for Pylgrymes" (sic) The various shrines sold badges for the pilgrims to collect and as additional proof that they had taken part in the pilgrimage. One of Canterbury's badges shows a sword passing through a mitre, indicating the way of St.Thomas's death, or a bishop riding on a donkey.

Visit: Canterbury - Chester - Chichester - Durham - Ely - Lincoln - Oxford - Rochester - St.Albans - Winchester.

'POOR MAN'S BIBLE' - at a time when most of the population was illiterate cathedrals and churches abounded in "illustrations", viz. carving, wallpaintings and stained glass in the windows. All these devices enabled the general populace to "read" the Bible through looking at the illustrations. "Look up here in the roof and see Adam and Eve in the Garden of Eden" etc. So the priest was able to explain the story of the Garden to his congregation.

PORCHES - originally little more than a "draught excluder" they were later used for a variety of purposes with chambers over them that could be used for meetings, or for lodgings for visiting clergy. In some cathedrals, Chichester - Ely - Durham they became known as "Galilee Porches" from the practice of reading part of the Palm Sunday Gospel from them. After the reading the bishop would knock on the west door with his crosier asking for entrance, and the entrance into Jerusalem.

Visit: Chelmsford - Chester - Chichester - Ely - Durham - Leicester.

PULPIT - a raised structure, made often of wood or stone, from which a sermon is delivered. All cathedrals have at least one, many have two or more, one in the choir area and the other in the nave.

Visit: Norwich and Winchester both have pulpits from the 15th century. Carlisle's is 16th century. Portsmouth and Wells have 17th century examples. Lincoln's is 18th century and came from Rotterdam, in Holland. York and St. Paul's London both possess pulpits of the 20th century. St.Paul's former pulpit is in the crypt and is a memorial to Captain Robert Fitzgerald of the Punjab Frontier Force, who died of sunstroke in 1853.

PULPITIUM - dividing the choir from the nave, i.e. monks from laity, a stone screen stretches across the cathedral. With doorways either side to provide for processions around the cathedral, the screen was often highly decorated with coloured statues off-setting the stonework.

Visit: Canterbury - Lincoln - Ripon - Rochester - York

REREDOS - against the east wall of the church, or attached to a free-standing altar is the reredos. Originally an elaborately embroidered woven cloth that has been replaced by either stone or woodwork with suitable carvings. Often the scene depicted is that of the Crucifixion of Christ with St.John the Evangelist and the Blessed Virgin Mary.

Visit; Chichester - with its tapestry designed by John Piper.
Coventry - has Graham Sutherland's "Christ in Majesty".
St. Albans - Southwark - Winchester have giant stone screens behind the high altar dating from the early 16th century.

RETABLE - is an "ornamental screenlike structure above and behind an altar" often with a ledge on which candles, and later crosses, would stand.

Visit: Norwich - the retable in the Lady Chapel dates from the 14th century.

ROBES - the use of linen robes in religious services is of early origin. In the Old Testament we read how "Samuel ministered before the Lord girded with a linen ephod". White robes were worn by the whole congregation in the early Church. Later those who were about to be baptised were dressed in white -a sign of purity. Similarly Confirmation candidates wore white on White Sunday (Whitsun). Today's white robes are the surplices, worn over a black or red cassock, and the long white alb under the eucharistic vestments. The black cassock, worn under the white surplice, was formerly an everyday dress of a Clerk in Holy Orders. The biretta, still worn by some clergy today, is a development from the Canterbury Cap of earlier times. Neither cassock nor cap are strictly speaking vestments but vestures that have been adopted by the clergy. In the Rubrics of 1549 the surplice was appointed to be worn by the clergy "in the saying of Mattins and Evensong, baptising and burying". Derived from the Latin *super-pelliceum* the garment worn over the *pelliceum*, a woollen or furred coat, the surplice today is usually made of white cotton or poly-cotton material. A Canon of 1604 directs that students in colleges should wear the surplice at the time of Divine Service. This is probably the origin of why members of the choir s wear surplices. The Rubrics of the First Prayer Book of 1549 reads " it is seemly, that graduates, when they preach, shall use such hoods as pertaineth to their several degrees".

ROMAN CATHOLIC CATHEDRALS - since the restoration of the Catholic Episcopate in 1850 there have been built a number of new cathedrals.

Visit: Birmingham (St. Chad) 1841 - Brentwood (Sacred Heart) 1869 - Cardiff (St. David) 1887 - Clifton (Holy Apostles) 1848 - Hexham and Newcastle (St. Mary) 1860 - Lancaster (St.Peter) 1859 - Leeds (St. Anne) 1904 - Liverpool, old (St.Nicholas) 1858 - Liverpool, new (Christ the King) 1967 - Menevia Wrexham (Our Lady of Dolours) 1907 - Middlesbrough (St. Mary) 1911 - Northampton (St. Mary and St. Thomas) 1864 - Nottingham (St.Barnabas) 1844 - Plymouth (St. Mary and St. Boniface) 1880 - Portsmouth (St.John the Evangelist) 1887 - Salford (St. John) 1890 - Shrewsbury (Our Lady Help of Christians and St.Peter of Alcantara) 1856 - Southwark (St. George) 1894 - Westminster (The Most Precious Blood) 1903 - Arundel (Our Lady and St.Philip) 1973.

ROOF BOSSES - the keystone at the intersection of the ribs of the vaulting that are very often carved with the most extra-ordinary carvings. To see and appreciate these fine works of art a good pair of binoculars is needed, although in some cathedrals a mirror on wheels is provided which saves the strain on the neck! These are indeed a "poor man's bible".
Visit: Canterbury - Norwich - Winchester - York (with its modern design example in the restored south transept following the disastrous fire of 1984 -look for the "Raising of the Mary Rose", "Famine relief" and "Save the Whales". These are three of the six prize-winning entries from a competition by BBC TV children's programme "Blue Peter". Some 32,000 children submitted designs).

ROOFS - either a timber structure or stone vaulting - in the case of the former often hammer or double hammer beam variety. Stone vaulting starts with the simple barrel vault of the 12th century and ends with the fan vault of the 15th century.

Visit: Durham - Gloucester - Lincoln - Norwich - Oxford - Peterborough - Salisbury -Southwark - York for vaulting.
Bury St. Edmunds - Ely - Leicester - Peterborough (nave) for timber roofs.

SANCTUARY - Until 1624 anybody wishing to evade custody by the Law could claim sanctuary, for up to thirty-seven days, in the cathedral. Many of the Closes became areas of sanctuary and were turned into ghettos of crime and vice - this did not please the other inhabitants! In places where only the church building was sanctuary, large knockers, - "sanctuary knockers", were attached to the main door of the church. By holding the knocker, when the church was closed, sanctuary could also be claimed.

Visit: Durham whose original knocker dating from the 12th century is now safe in the cathedral's library/museum. A replica has been attached to the door on the north-west corner of the church. The porch, demolished in the eighteenth century by James Wyatt during his "restoration" of the building, was used to house "serten men dyd lie alwaises in two chambers over the said north door, that any offender dyd come and knocke, straight waie they were letten in, at any hour of the nyght".

SCHOOLS - the Benedictine Order has always put strong emphasis on teaching. Many of the Benedictine abbeys/cathedrals had schools, and this is continued today with various cathedral choir schools. Bury St.Edmunds and Ely both had schools in the 7th century. Edward the Confessor, King of England, was a pupil at the latter.

SCREENS - are used to partition off parts of the building making small, more convenient areas for worship. There are often screens around the choir area those at Winchester have chests balanced along the top and are said to contain the bones of ancient worthies, bishops, saints and kings of Wessex. Replacing the pulpitium of medieval days is the choir screen of the 19th century, manly the work of Sir George Gilbert Scott, and erected at the time of his restoration of the cathedrals. At Coventry there is a hanging screen of glass at the "west" end of the new cathedral building, with effigies of saints etched on it.

SERVICES ARE FOR ALL ! - there is a regular pattern of daily worship in all the cathedrals commencing with Holy Communion usually about 8 a.m. with Mattins (Morning Prayer) following later in the morning and the day ends with Evening Prayer in the late afternoon. Visitors are always welcome to attend these services, and are often directed to sit up in the choir area. It must, however, be realised that from time to time the church is required for special, "ticket only", events such as memorial services, or special invitation services. On these occasions ticket holders will obviously be given preference - but even then the cathedral authorities may have allowed space, usually at the back, for those who may wish to attend the service. Never walk away - just make a judicious enquiry!

SHOP AND BOOKSTALL - you may have bought this book from the cathedral bookstall, in which case it is irrelevant to suggest a visit, but you can always return for a second look (and buy?). All the profit from the bookstall and its attendant shop will help the cathedral's finances.

SHRINES - containing the relics of saints shrines were often the focal point of the cathedral and were normally found behind the high altar. As they were the object of pilgrimages they brought considerable wealth not only to the cathedral but also to the city. Pilgrims have to be fed, provided with beds, and their general welfare cared for in the most hospitable way possible. At the time of the Refor- mation most shrines were destroyed and in many cases only very scant remains have been found and re-assembled on the site of the original shrine. The following places have some remnants, and for convenience the saint's feast day is given enabling the reader to visit the shrine on his/her day.

19th January	Worcester	St. Wulstan
3rd February	Chester	St. Werberga
19th February	Worcester	St. Oswald
6th March	Peterborough	St. Tibba
19th March	Derby	St. Alkmund
20th March	Durham	St. Cuthbert
3rd April	Chichester	St. Richard
23rd May	Rochester	St. William
27th May	Durham	St. Bede
22nd June	St. Albans	St. Alban
15th July	Winchester	St. Swithun
19th October	Oxford	St. Frideswide
17th November	Lincoln	St. Hugh
4th December	Salisbury	St. Osmund
29th December	Canterbury	St. Thomas

Shrine of St. Ethelreda, Ely.

STAFF -

Dean — head of the Chapter and has overall responsibility for business etc., of the cathedral.

Precentor — oversees the music, ensuring that the note is pitched correctly.

Chancellor — acts as secretary to the Chapter and is responsible for education, particularly for cathedral schools and the cathedral's library. He shares, with the Precentor, the appointment of readers, teachers, etc.

Treasurer — is the "Keeper of the Cathedral Treasures". In earlier times he had to pay for the repair of all damages to them out of his own pocket. To counter this his income was considerably larger than his colleagues of the Chapter. In a medieval manuscript the duties of the Treasurer take up four pages, the Dean one, and the Chancellor one paragraph.

Prebendary — a "prebend" is a piece of land, income from which paid the prebendary his salary until 1836 when the Ecclesiastical Commissioners (Church Commissioners) took over the responsibility.

Canons — similar to the prebendary and similarly paid.

Virgers/Vergers — an ecclesiastical official who carries a wand or mace in front of a Senior church official.

Wandsmen — act as ushers for the main services of the cathedral, usually they are retired persons who give their services voluntarily. Some cathedrals "dress" them in gowns, while others prefer them in morning dress.

STAINED GLASS - another of the "visual-aids" to prayer and meditation - the glass in the windows with the earliest piece in situ being in the great west window of Canterbury Cathedral. It shows Adam digging in the Garden of Eden. The cathedral has the greatest treasury of stained glass of all the cathedrals of England. At Ely there is, in the triforium, a Museum of Stained Glass with examples from medieval to modern times. It was opened in 1972 since when it has been visited by countless people who have been intrigued with both the displays and the rescue work undertaken for glass no longer wanted. In the north transept of Lincoln Cathedral can be seen the "Dean's Eye' that is made up of 13th century stained glass.

STATUES - abounded in medieval cathedrals, as in parish churches, but the iconoclasts of the 16th and 17th centuries destroyed most of them. Today they can be seen both inside and outside the cathedrals once more.

Visit:		
	Blackburn	John Hayward's "Christ the Worker"
	Chelmsford	Huxley Jones' "St. Peter the Fisherman"
	Coventry	Epstein's "Michael the Archangel"
	Guildford	Eric Gill's "The Blessed Trinity"
	Manchester	Sir Charles Wheeler's "Madonna" dressed as a mill girl
	Peterborough	Alan Durst's renewal of the statuary on the West Front. Look for the head of H.M. the Queen
	Winchester	Statue of James I and Charles I once on a screen, also a 14th century "Madonna"

St. Augustine. From the Door of the Chapter House, Rochester.

TOMBS - burial places for the mighty as well as the humble and meek. Surrounding the cathedral building can be seen, and visited, the graves of some of the past worshippers at the church. Stop and read some of the epitaphs. It will be a worthwhile exercise. Strictly speaking a grave is a place of burial, and a tomb a monument erected over the grave. In the early Middle Ages bodies were either buried in the ground, or in stone coffins. Later a Law was issued enforcing all to be buried in a woollen shroud. Today many cathedrals will only accept cremated ashes for interment in the cathedral.

Visit: Canterbury - with many of the former Archbishops, including the last Roman Catholic, viz. Cardinal Reginald Pole. The Black Prince and, of course, St. Thomas Becket.
Derby - Bess of Hardwick, who outlived four husbands and was the founder of the Devonshire Family.
Durham - St. Bede and St. Cuthbert.
Ely - Alan of Walsingham, the architect of the lantern here.
Norwich - Nurse Cavell, shot as a spy in the First World War.
Peterborough - here were Catherine of Aragon Henry VIII's wife, and Mary, Queen of Scots, later re-interred in Westminster Abbey.
Southwark - John Gower - the first English Poet.
Winchester - St. Swithun, Jane Austen, and William Rufus.
Worcester - King John and Prince Henry.

 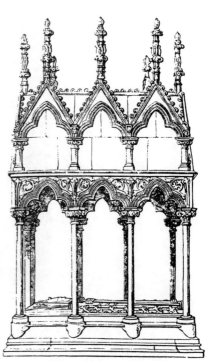

Tomb of Aymer de Valence. Westminster Abbey.   Tomb of Archbishop Grey. York Cathedral.

TOWERS AND SPIRES - a dictionary definition of a tower is " a building of considerable elevation" and a spire " a tower tapering to a point" while a steeple is " a spire with bells in it ". Only two cathedrals have triple spires - Lichfield whose west ones date from the 14th century as did the central spire that was destroyed and rebuilt in the 17th century. The other is Truro all of whose spires date from the 19th century. Norwich, whose original spire was blown down in a gale was replaced by the present one at the end of the 15th century. Salisbury's spire was completed in 1334 and contains within it the medieval scaffolding, with a fragment of the robe of the Blessed Virgin Mary sealed in a leaden box at the top.   Up to the 18th century, at the time of the James Wyatt " ruthless restoration", a free-standing bell tower stood close by the church. By reputation Oxford's spire is the oldest surviving example in England, dating from the 13th century.

Visit: Chester - a free-standing bell tower was completed in 1974.
Chichester - central tower (13th century) with a 19th century rebuilt spire.
Ely - west tower (14th century) with central lantern rebuilt in 1322 by Alan of Walsingham.
Exeter - tower either end of transepts (12th century).
Newcastle - 15th century lantern tower with steeple held in place by a crown of flying buttresses.
Portsmouth - central tower 1691 with 1703 cupola.
St. Albans - central tower constructed from Roman tiles from Verulamium.
Southwell - twin west towers with Rhenish caps.
Wakefield - with its 15th century crocketted spire.
York - all three towers date from the 15th century.
(south west 1456 - north-west 1474 - central 1480)

Lichfield. General View.

TREASURY - here is displayed the plate, chalices, patens, almsdishes, ciboriums, and the vestments of the church.

Cup found in the Ruins of Glastonbury Abbey.

Visit: Chichester - Norwich - St. Paul's London.

UNDERCROFT - strictly speaking an undercroft is a crypt with windows, both words are used to describe a below ground room.

VESTMENTS - in the First Book of Common Prayer (1549) in the reign of Edward VI the vestment and cope are particularly referred to under the heading "the ornaments of the church", shall be "retained and used". In the second book it is expressively ordered that one or other of these vestures shall be worn by the priest upon all occasions of the "ministration of the holy communion". Later, in the 17th century, these robes were considered "papist" and they fell out of use. In the 19th century at the time of the Oxford/Tractarian Movement they were fully restored to use - but not by all clerics. As with the colours of the altar frontals each season of the church has its own colour of vestments.

VISITING CATHEDRALS - many people have come to look upon the great cathedrals as being museums but it should be remembered that their prime function is to act as a place of worship to Almighty God. Voices should be kept at a low key in order not to disturb other visitors and those who may wish to offer prayer during their visit to the cathedral.

WATCHING LOFTS - guarded the shrines of the saints in order to keep an eye on the pilgrims! Stealing from churches, and shrines, was not unheard of in medieval times !

Visit: Oxford - St.Albans.

WEST FRONT - usually the main entrance to the cathedral, but not necessarily the one by which the visitor enters the church. Its importance is reflected in its grandeur with elaborate carvings, etc.

Visit: Bath & Wells - Bury St. Edmunds - Canterbury - Coventry (new church with its great glass screen) - Exeter - Lincoln - Peterborough - Rochester - St. Paul's, London - Salisbury - York.